I AM A
SISTER NOW

This book belongs to

Mommy and Daddy and little Eileen
Were all just as happy as happy could be
They played and they cuddled and every day
When Mommy put Eileen to bed she would say:

I love you so much, you light up my life.

I'll see you tomorrow - but for now, good night!"

One day at the park in the middle of spring
Mommy and Daddy sat down with Eileen

They said, ***"We have got just the biggest surprise!"***
And Eileen perked up with a spark in her eye.

Could it be a present, or maybe ice cream?
She was so OVERWHELMED by what could-it-be's!

ZOO
LOVE

Could it be a puppy, with big puppy eyes?
Could it be a princess gown, made just her size?
Were they taking a trip to the blue monkey zoo?

She wondered and wondered, what else could she do?
Every second she waited felt like forever.
What in the world would her mom and dad tell her?

"You may notice that some things have changed in the house
Mommy's wearing new clothes, and the spare room is cleaned out

Well, the reason for that, we're excited to say,
Is that you have a baby sister on the way!

She's growing inside Mommy's belly today
And in just a few months she will be here to stay!"

All of a sudden, to Eileen's surprise,
Eileen felt hot tears welling up in her eyes.
Her tummy felt bad, jumbled all up in knots,
And her feelings were so big she thought she might pop.
She couldn't explain, and she couldn't say why,
But she let out a scream and she started to cry.

That night when her parents put Eileen to bed
They told her the same thing
they always had said:

"I love you so much, you light up my life.
I'll see you tomorrow - but for now,
good night!"

But try as she might, and try as she may,
Eileen's big bad feeling still kept her awake.

Eileen watched each day as her Mommy and Daddy
Filled up Baby's room with toys and diaper caddies
They still liked to cuddle with Eileen and play
And Eileen saw mom's belly get bigger each day!
Daddy put Eileen's old crib in the room
Where her new baby sister would come to stay soon.

Eileen felt all mixed up by all of this change
Was anything going to remain the same?
It's true, she was too old for her baby crib
But that old crib was HERS, even if she's too big!
So sometimes Eileen slipped away by herself
To sit in her room with the feeling she felt.

But at the same time, Eileen knew that her friends
Loved their siblings a lot. So she couldn't pretend
That there wasn't a part of herself that was eager
To say hi to her sister and finally meet her!
She felt all these mixed feelings come up inside
But she couldn't explain, and she couldn't say why.

One day after school, Eileen got picked up
Not by Mommy or Daddy, but Grandma's big truck!
"I'm taking you home," she explained to Eileen,
"Because Mommy has gone into labor, which means
That in not very long, maybe even today,
You'll see your new sister! Does that not sound great?"

Eileen felt her belly get filled up with feelings
For the whole ride home Eileen feel quite queasy
She wondered if her Mom and Dad were okay
At the hospital, which just seemed so far away
That night, Grandma had to put Eileen to bed
In the morning, Eileen got up having gotten no rest

But just as Grandma was setting out their breakfast,
The front door went screeee - and Eileen saw her parents!
And what was that, wrapped up in little white clothes?
Eileen's baby sister - she'd made it back home!
Mommy gave Eileen a big hug and kiss,
And said, ***"Would you like to hold your baby sis?"***

Eileen looked at the little red face in the bundle
So fragile and small it made her tummy tumble.
Eileen shook her head and took one step away.
What if she somehow made an awful mistake?
Mommy and Daddy just nodded and smiled.
"Maybe we'll try again in just a little while."

“Mommy is tired, so she’s going to sleep,”
Said Daddy, explaining to little Eileen,
“She has to wake up when the new baby needs her,
And also her body has been through the ringer!
So just for now, let’s both leave Mommy alone
And I’ll take care of everything else here at home.”

Before Eileen could ask her dad any questions,
Everyone ran off in different directions.

Mommy and baby
took naps in their beds,

Daddy prepped food for
their dinnertime spread.

Grandma drove her big
truck on back to her home,

And Eileen sat in the living room alone.

She thought to herself - hey, this doesn't seem right!
She'd just been away from her parents all night!
She'd been worried sick - and did nobody care?
They might as well act like Eileen wasn't there!
At least that's what Eileen thought must be the case
But she tried her hardest to keep a straight face.

The more that she thought, the more that she stewed,
The more the big bad feelings in herself grew.
She couldn't explain, and she couldn't say why,
But her body let out a loud, blood-curdling cry
Then across the house, with little delay,
The baby cried too, like a little freight train!

Eileen closed her mouth almost right away
But by that time it was already too late.
***"Eileen, you know you need to remain quiet!
Your mom and the baby both need
to have silence."***
She could tell from her dad's voice
that he was annoyed,
And Eileen felt a guilt that
she couldn't avoid.

She wondered and wondered why she felt so bad.
She thought a big sister like her should be glad.
She worried that maybe something had gone wrong
Inside of herself, and she mused all day long
Until finally Daddy said, ***"It's time for bed.***
Mom and I won't be long, so just go on ahead."

And all of a sudden Eileen felt much better!
Soon enough she and Mom and Dad would be together.

So she brushed her own teeth and put on her own jammies.

And got into her bed and
felt cozy and happy.

She looked at the clock
while she waited for them
To tell her goodnight
and put her to bed.

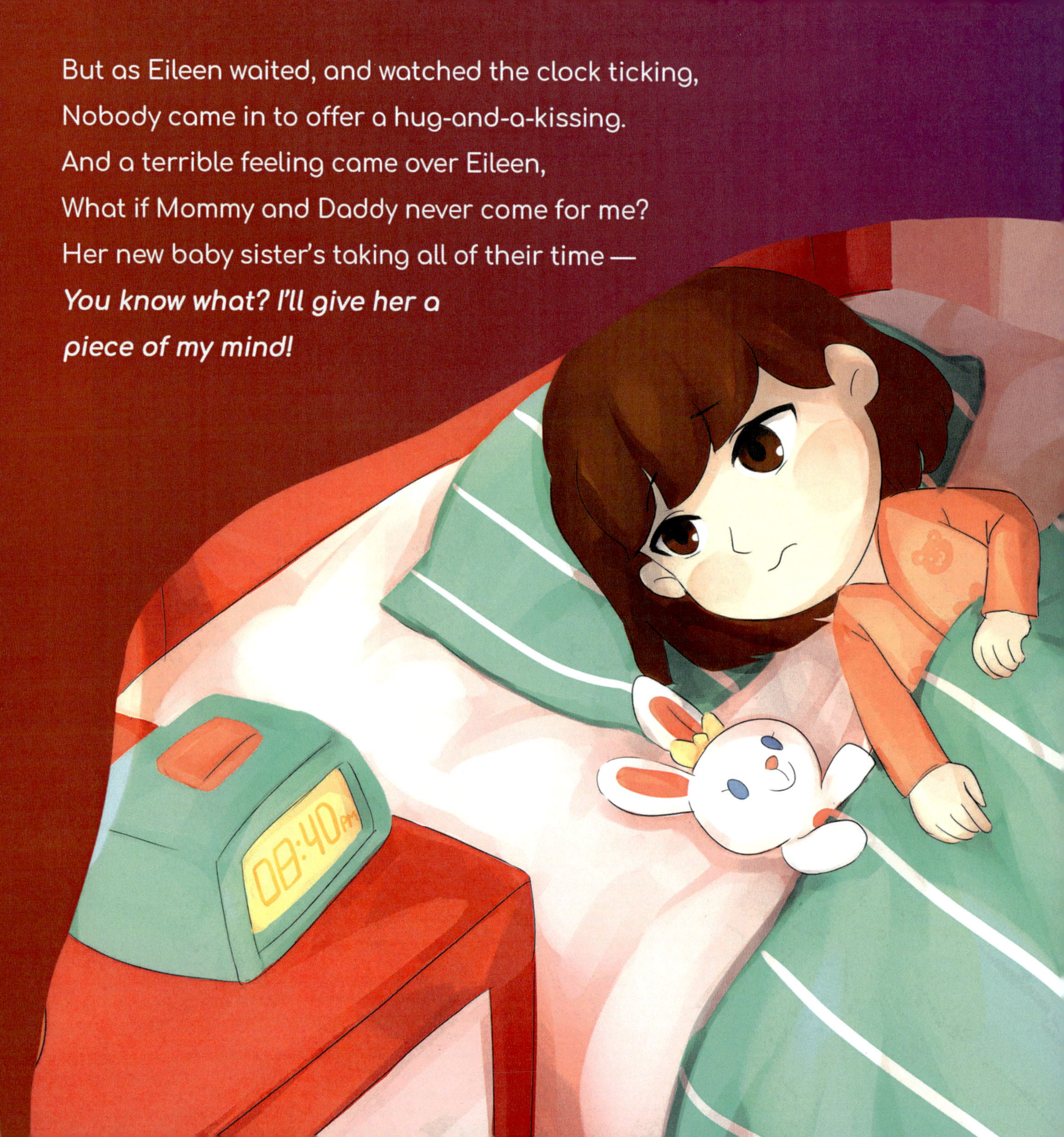

But as Eileen waited, and watched the clock ticking,
Nobody came in to offer a hug-and-a-kissing.
And a terrible feeling came over Eileen,
What if Mommy and Daddy never come for me?
Her new baby sister's taking all of their time —
You know what? I'll give her a
piece of my mind!

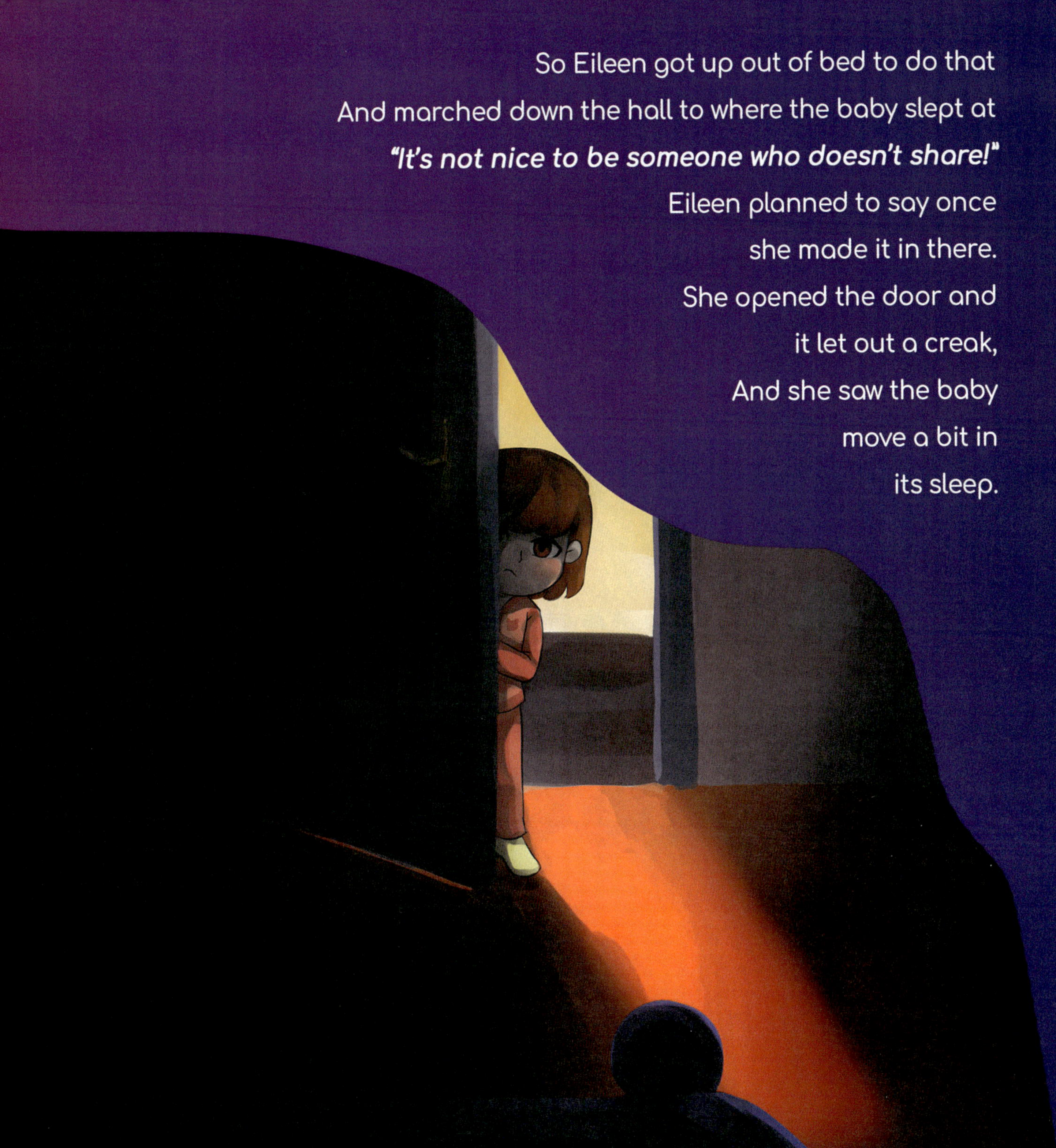

So Eileen got up out of bed to do that
And marched down the hall to where the baby slept at
"It's not nice to be someone who doesn't share!"
Eileen planned to say once
she made it in there.
She opened the door and
it let out a creak,
And she saw the baby
move a bit in
its sleep.

Up to the crib went Eileen, super-fast,
but when she got there,
Eileen stopped in her tracks
The baby in white looked
so cute and so pretty,
and suddenly Eileen felt awfully silly
A baby's a baby, and Eileen knew that,
but what else could she do with
these feelings she had?

Out of the blue, Eileen saw a light
Eileen's parents, behind her, both let out big sighs
"We both got so worried, you weren't in your bed!
We're so glad to see that you're safe here instead."
When Eileen saw her parents, tears filled up her eyes
And she let loose the feelings she's tried hard to hide.

"I've had this big feeling inside of my tummy
And it makes my whole body and head feel so yucky.
Ever since you said that I'd be a big sister
It keeps getting worse, getting bigger and bigger!
And now you won't like me the way that you did,
Because I'm a big baby and not a big kid."

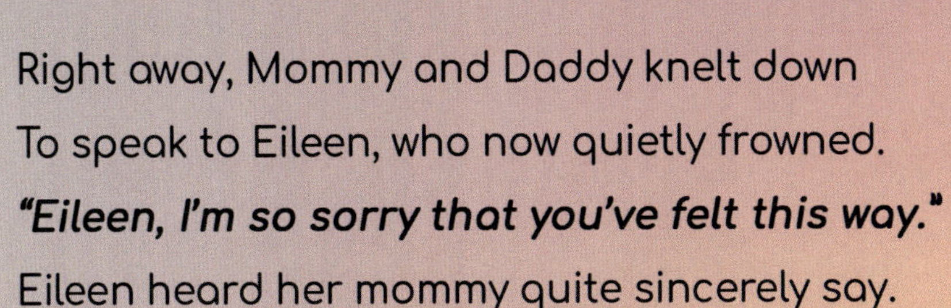

Right away, Mommy and Daddy knelt down
To speak to Eileen, who now quietly frowned.
"Eileen, I'm so sorry that you've felt this way."
Eileen heard her mommy quite sincerely say.
"I'm glad that you're telling us now how you feel,
And I know that the feelings you're having are real."

“There’s nothing you can ever say, feel or do
That will ever make Mommy and me not love you.
I can’t read your mind, but I can make a guess -
That big bad dark feeling is called “loneliness”.
Right now, me and mom have to take care of the baby
And have a bit less time to spend with you, maybe.”

"But it won't be long until your little sister
Starts to walk and to talk and get bigger and bigger!
And all of the things you love doing with us -
Playing and cuddling and having great fun -
Will be things that we can all do as a group
And that baby will love you as much as we do."

Eileen imagined all this as he spoke
Playing princess together, sharing funny jokes.
And the bad feeling that had been in her so long
Started to fade, and new feelings came strong,
Like a brand-new excitement for getting to know
Her new little sister, and helping her grow.

"How about right now we do this together,"
Said Mommy, who could tell that Eileen felt better,
"Let's all say good night to each other and Baby
The same way we say good night now to you daily
I'd love you to help me to put her to bed,
And then we'll say goodnight to you, sleepyhead!"

So Mommy and Daddy and little Eileen,
Who were all just as happy as happy could be,
Leaned in towards the crib, all whispering low.
They all knew by heart the way the words go:
"I love you so much,
you light up my life.
I'll see you tomorrow,
but for now, good night!"